Customer Experience

365

Roy Andrew Barnes

Customer Experience 365

DEDICATION

To those of you who deliver awesome
service every day!

CONTENTS

ACKNOWLEDGMENTS

A sincere thank you is due to our clients around the world. Their ongoing perseverance to embed customer experience as part of their culture inspired this book.

Special thanks Kimberly, Robin, Terry and Scott for your encouragement to get this done.

Finally, thanks to Jill, Evan, Casey, Caleb, Amelia and Abby for your brilliant insights and support.

INTRODUCTION

This book is about building tactical skill in providing exceptional customer experience. There's nothing academic, theoretical, or complicated here—just practical daily guidance on how to get better in service delivery.

Great customer experience is all about consistency—making it happen at every interaction, every single day. While delivering occasional random acts of exceptional customer service is nice, it isn't the objective. Consistent performance is about repetition. It's about training the mind and muscle to react perfectly and instinctually to any situation that may occur.

For those of you with children (or who were once children), think about the process of teaching a kid how to properly use his or her eating utensils. It isn't a tell 'em once process. It is an every day, every meal process. If you're lucky, by the time the kid starts eating in public, he or she has built the behavioral memory necessary to make eating with utensils automatic. That's kind of what we're shooting for here: instinctive service.

Any individual, manager, supervisor, or anyone else who leads a team of customer-facing employees can use customer *Experience 365*. Please share each day's entry to provide a regular reminder at standup meetings, shift meetings, or "dock talks". Read the daily advice out loud, ask for a real-world example that relates to the topic, or just inquire how team members might execute that advice in their upcoming interactions. Whatever approach you take, we promise you'll deliver better customer experience!

JANUARY

JANUARY 1

At the start of each customer interaction, smile. Be the first one to do so. Set the tone. How you start a conversation will determine its course and success. Don't wait for the other person. You're in charge of how this exchange will turn out.

JANUARY 2

Decide that you will own the resolution of any inquiry, problem, or concern that your customer raises. That means no hand-offs, no passing the buck, and no ducking responsibility. If you need to involve others to solve the problem, do so. But *you* must remain responsible for following up with the customer personally.

JANUARY 3

Manage the first impression. Imagine
you are an actor walking on stage for
the first time. You have just three
seconds to create an impression. In the
first moments of any customer
interaction, the customer is assessing his
or her like or dislike of you. Use those
precious first moments very wisely.

JANUARY 4

Don't just look at your customers. *See* them. You aren't just engaging in a transaction; you are establishing or deepening a human connection. Every customer interaction should strengthen that relationship. You are always building relations or weakening them. There is no neutral.

JANUARY 5

You are an emotion-creating machine. When you are with others, whether at work or at home, you are creating emotion and feeling inside of them. What people remember about you now is based on how you made them feel during your last interaction with them.

JANUARY 6

Your eyes transmit your intentions. That means no sunglasses, no long bangs, and no hat brims hanging low over your face. Don't let anything block your customers' view of your eyes. Let them see you.

JANUARY 7

If you find yourself losing patience, physically step away from the interaction if at all possible. Even a five-second break can help to calm you down a little. The trick is to interrupt your trajectory, even if just for a moment. Simply say a polite "Excuse me for just a moment," back away, and take a breath.

JANUARY 8

How many times should you apologize to a customer? As many times as it takes. Remove your ego from every single one of your customer interactions. Even though it will rarely be your fault that a customer is upset, don't be afraid to say "I'm sorry."

JANUARY 9

Can you anticipate what your customer will ask of you next? If so, why wait for him or her to ask? Always lead when you know the path. Being on the receiving end of someone who anticipates your needs is pretty great!

JANUARY 10

It takes courage to be of service to customers when other employees around you aren't. Human beings naturally tend to exhibit the behaviors of the broader group to which they belong. Either lead your work team in the creation of a new attitude or leave. Whatever you do, don't let your spirit to serve be diminished by any knuckleheads around you.

JANUARY 11

Receiving praise is a rare event in most people's lives. A heartfelt acknowledgement from one co-worker to another can change lives. Within the next few hours, find someone who is being of good service to others and thank him or her.

JANUARY 12

Allow upset customers to discharge their anger with no interruption from you. Don't defend yourself, don't make excuses, and don't cut in. *Zippen-zee-lippen!* When you're dealing with an unhappy customer, it's time for you to be quiet. Think of it this way: If you were going to ventilate a room to remove dangerous fumes, you'd open the doors and windows and stand back. Do the same thing with angry customers. Give them space to vent, and you'll find it much easier to resolve their problem.

JANUARY 13

Beware "the stack." Often, a customer won't have had just one thing go wrong. Sometimes, two or three things will have stacked up. And like the final straw that broke the camel's back, that last problem will be the one that pushes the customer over the edge. When faced with such a customer, take time to listen. Then make sure you ask enough clarifying questions to uncover all the customer's issues and concerns. Solving just one problem won't cut it if the customer has five more issues they are upset about!

JANUARY 14

Use the customer's name whenever possible. Not only is it respectful, but there are very few people who don't like hearing their own name. Personalizing an interaction by referring to someone by name is a great trick to both calm people down and boost them up.

JANUARY 15

Document customer issues and problems right away. Don't wait to write down details about a customer's problem and the steps you took to solve it. Sure, adding this type of information to a customer database is a pain in the neck, but the data you add today can keep similar problems from reoccurring tomorrow.

JANUARY 16

Every customer interaction creates emotion, either positive or negative. Each interaction also creates expectation in the customer's mind of what will happen next. Your job is to provide clear direction to your customer about what he or she can expect to happen next. Don't ever let customers get confused or lost in the sequence of upcoming events.

JANUARY 17

You really can't make directions simple enough for everyone to understand. Some customers understand things better in writing, some customers prefer to learn from drawings, and a lucky few understand complex ideas in just a few spoken words. When you're explaining something to a customer, it is best to try all three approaches. Aim as if you're trying to explain it to a not-so-bright fifth grader, and you'll probably hit it about right.

JANUARY 18

If a customer asks where something is located, if it is at all practical, escort him or her there yourself.

JANUARY 19

Modifying the pace at which you speak
can give you control in a conversation. If
a customer is very upset and talking
quickly, don't match his or her pace.
Slow your responses just a little, and
you'll find that the customer will often
calm down, too.

JANUARY 20

When faced with an angry customer, become human to him or her as quickly as possible. It is easier for a customer to be mad at some large, faceless company than with the human being standing across from him or her. Right off the bat, introduce yourself with your first name and your role and tell the customer you want to help solve his or her problem, issue, or concern right now.

JANUARY 21

You might not be aware of it, but your customer is paying very close attention to your facial expressions. Customers always look for signs of acceptance and openness from you. Your inattentiveness and obvious boredom is like a siren screaming in the customer's mind, "He doesn't care about me or my problem!" Pay attention to the small details of your presence.

JANUARY 22

Are you on a phone, radio, or intercom during the course of your workday? If so, smile. Customers can hear it in your voice. As a reminder, put a small mirror by your phone. When you see your smile, they'll hear the difference.

JANUARY 23

Today, at least one of your customers will be going through a rough patch in his or her life. Maybe that customer is going through a divorce, just lost a job, just started a diet, just had a car accident, or just lost a loved one. Whatever it is the customer is dealing with, the attitude you bring to the interaction can entirely change his or her outlook.

JANUARY 24

Don't talk trash about another department, division, employee, or other area of your company. To the customer, you are one organization. The customer doesn't care about your office politics or who has the boss's ear, power, or influence. In your interactions today, *you* are the face of the company. You are the brand, you are the logo, and you are responsible for the reputation of the entire team.

JANUARY 25

How do your internal customers feel
about the level of customer experience
they get from you? You know who
we're talking about, right? We mean the
employees in other departments who
depend on you. These internal
customers deserve the same level of
attention and care as your external ones.

JANUARY 26

How you say something is almost as important as what you actually say. Tone of voice really matters!

JANUARY 27

Learn to apologize. Things are going to go wrong. Although it's hard to predict what will go wrong, it's easy to say "I'm sorry" when it does. When done with a tone of real sincerity, nothing beats a great apology (well, other than not screwing things up in the first place).

JANUARY 28

How you begin and end a customer interaction matters more than what happened in the middle. Start strong and finish strong. Your customers will remember your last words and actions.

JANUARY 29

Your customer's experience with you is like a story. It has a beginning, a middle, and an end. Your job is to be the author — the creative director — of that story and of the customer's experience. What is the outcome of the story you're going to write today?

JANUARY 30

Don't have a transactional mindset—for example, "We're here to do a job then get out as fast as possible." Your objective is to foster conversation with customers by reaching past the transaction and engaging with them as people. This doesn't take much time. It just takes you exhibiting an interest in your customers and their needs.

JANUARY 31

You want as much customer feedback as you can possibly get. It doesn't matter if it's good or bad. The more information you can get from your customers about how they perceive your products and services, the better. Every complaint is a gift that you can use to improve.

FEBRUARY

FEBRUARY 1

Customers get lost when you use too much technical jargon, terms, and explanations. Be on the lookout for customer confusion. If you're paying attention, you'll see it in their eyes or the expression on their face. Don't hesitate to stop and ask, "Am I being clear on what I'm trying to explain?"

FEBRUARY 2

Great ideas, great products, and great services are not good enough. People want a connection. They want a real, live, caring human being who will take the time to listen, learn, and help. Despite what your job description says, this is your *real* job.

FEBRUARY 3

Don't practice on your customers.
Whether it's refining your marketing
message, improving your customer
service, changing your product, or
enhancing your service, get it right
before you release it into the customer's
environment.

FEBRUARY 4

Customer experience, by the numbers:

- Five percent of people deliver great customer experience.
- Thirty percent pay lip service to it.
- Sixty-five percent don't believe it matters at all.

Where are you, really?

FEBRUARY 5

Here are four great questions to ask your customers today:

- How can I help you?
- Can you tell me more about…?
- What do you mean by…?
- I heard you say…. Did I get it right?

FEBRUARY 6

If your customer could provide a one-word answer to the question, "What was it *really* like to interact with you today?" what would his or her answer be?

FEBRUARY 7

More than half of a customer's experience has nothing to do with the product. Rather, it has to do with how you made him or her feel.

FEBRUARY 8

Even though they won't admit it, most people aren't just buying a product. They are buying an emotional state of mind. Everything is an emotional buy of some kind. Everything.

FEBRUARY 9

Are you scary? Focus on putting your customer at ease. Introduce yourself (share your name, not just your company's). Try to make the customer feel comfortable. Build rapport. Ask what the customer does, what his or her interests are, whether he or she has kids, and so on.

FEBRUARY 10

Asking questions is not annoying. It shows interest on your part. Ask, and then listen intently. Focus on the details of what the customer is saying and probe for more information. Don't assume you know the answer. Test your attentiveness.

FEBRUARY 11

Generally speaking, people prefer visual descriptors to words. Get out a paper and pencil and become an artist. Give the customer a pencil and let him or her draw, too.

FEBRUARY 12

Hold a "pain-storming" session with three or four other employees in your area. Ask, "What are the customer's pain points for which we can provide relief?" Is there anything you can do immediately to fix their most common problems? If so, then do it.

FEBRUARY 13

A customer's experience is the sum total of all the interactions that he or she has with you and the rest of your organization. If you see others letting the customer down, step up and say something. Each and every interaction has to be great, not just yours.

FEBRUARY 14

Although it might not be fair, customers carry their experiences (good and bad) from one transaction to the next — even when those transactions are with other companies. If the local pizza delivery guys gave your customer outstanding personalized service during their last interaction, your customer is going to expect that from you, too.

FEBRUARY 15

Are you clear on what your customer experience intent is? Customer experience intent is simply a declaration of what you (or your company) want your customers to experience in every interaction. So, what do you want them to feel?

FEBRUARY 16

Who in your organization do customers typically deal with before they interact with you? Are you and your fellow employees all on the same page in terms of what you want the customer's experience to be? Set up a quick meeting and talk to that person or team about what's working and what isn't.

FEBRUARY 17

How is the quality of your customer interactions measured? How do you know that you're getting better at delivering the experience you intend? The best judge of experience is not you. It's the customer. Ask them directly what they think.

FEBRUARY 18

Criticism is tough to hear. These days, the Internet, social media, and other channels make it pretty easy for people to tear others down. If you hear negative comments about your service, personality, or whatever, decide whether the feedback is serious and thoughtful. If so, take it to heart and learn from it. Everything else, you should take with a grain of salt.

FEBRUARY 19

Your ability to move and change things is more significant than you might imagine. Your words, actions, and perspective *do* move others to change their behaviors and attitudes. A well-intentioned remark, comment, or observation can change the trajectory of your customer's day.

FEBRUARY 20

Most employees are paid to focus on just their discrete slice of the business. For example, they might get paid to make your company's processes more lean, efficient, or whatever. Customers, however, don't care about these internal issues. They care about their experiences with you.

If you want to put yourself in the customer's shoes, you have to take yours off first. In your next conversation with a customer, stop reacting from an "inside-the-company" perspective. Try to see the situation from the customer's vantage point.

FEBRUARY 21

One out of every four customers has gotten shuffled from one person to another in the same company without any resolution of their problem. It's easy to hand off a customer. Don't. Fix the customer's problem for him or her now.

FEBRUARY 22

In a grocery store, customers can smell the flowers, listen to the music, press the top of a cantaloupe to assess its ripeness, eyeball that carton of eggs for any broken ones, taste the food samples, and even squeeze the Charmin. Retailers know that when you touch something, you're more likely to buy it. Customers are multi-sensory creatures. How can you engage more of your customers' senses during their interactions with you?

FEBRUARY 23

An interested competitor can copy almost every part of your company's product and service offering. Your individual ability to offer awesome customer experience can't be so easily duplicated. When it comes right down to it, *you* are what differentiates your company from the rest.

FEBRUARY 24

Great customer experience isn't:

- Inconsistent
- Transactional
- Emotionless
- Boring
- Unplanned

FEBRUARY 25

If given a choice, seventy percent of customers would leave your business for another due to poor customer service. The importance of the relative quality of your actual products and services is a distant second, at just over ten percent. Customer service and experience matter to your customers. In some cases, it's even more important than the product or service you sell.

FEBRUARY 26

Satisfaction is not the end game. Rather, an engaging customer experience is the objective you should be aiming for. Satisfaction is table stakes. It's what you have to do just to play the game. If all you're doing is satisfying your customers, you shouldn't be in business.

FEBRUARY 27

Customers are becoming more and more demanding. They expect you to leap tall buildings in a single bound to fix their problem immediately. Not every customer is fun to deal with, but Superman didn't save people based on their personality. Time to put your cape on and serve everyone equally well.

FEBRUARY 28

Before you respond to a customer who is voicing a concern or complaint, take an extra second or two to ask a few clarifying questions to get to the bottom of the situation. That way, you can be sure you're solving the *real* problem.

FEBRUARY 29

Leap with enthusiasm into every interaction. Decide that you're going to be the one who manages and controls how engaging this experience is going to be. Don't wait!

MARCH

MARCH 1

Standard responses to problems feel like just that: standard. Any customer who is feeling the sting of some problem you or your organization has caused feels that pain as an individual. If the answer is a canned "We know this is a problem but we can't be bothered to fix it" response, the customer's experience will worsen quickly. Act as if the customer's issue is unique and deal with as if it is the first time it has ever happened.

MARCH 2

In every interaction with a customer today, ask yourself these three questions:

- What is the customer feeling right now?
- What is he or she trying to get done?
- What can I do to improve what the customer is feeling?

MARCH 3

Become the customer, if even just for today. Do what customers do, see what they see, and hear what they hear. Walk through all the steps that you and your company force them to take. This is called *walking the path*. Do it, and you'll discover some really whacked-out hoops that you're requiring the customer to jump through.

MARCH 4

No matter what part of your organization you work in, go look at your company's website (not your intranet site). If a customer wanted to find you or someone on your team for assistance, could he or she do so easily?

MARCH 5

Your organization's website should be structured for your customer's ease of use, not as a company bulletin board. Can a customer navigate around with ease? Is anything confusing? Is everything that has to do with your part of the customer experience correct, easy to use, and up to date? If not, fix it

MARCH 6

Nothing destroys customer experience like getting shuffled between departments, agents, or different levels of customer support. Ask yourself, is there anything you can do to address the customer's needs, concerns, or problems in just one call, one email, or one text? One-stop solutions are optimal.

MARCH 7

In your organization, the business or performance measures related to customer experience should be highly visible. In addition, employees should be held accountable for delivering specific, targeted results. Do you have customer performance targets? How are you and your team doing at achieving them?

MARCH 8

Successful organizations create a balanced set of measures:

- **Employee metrics:** How engaged are the other employees you work with?
- **Process metrics:** How well are you managing your business processes in terms of leanness and efficiency?
- **Customer metrics:** Are you delivering the intended customer experience?
- **Financial metrics:** Are you meeting or exceeding your department's or enterprise's financial performance targets?

To sustain a business for the long term, each of these four areas must be simultaneously managed well.

MARCH 9

Awesome customer experience is an outcome. It is the result of lots of different processes, behaviors, and attitudes across your entire organization. You must do your part, and so should everyone else.

For organizations that operate in silos, it is almost impossible to offer a holistic customer experience. Break down some intra-company walls. Visit another department and find out what they're doing to improve customer experience.

MARCH 10

Do you understand what customer experience success looks like in your specific job? Do you understand all the measures of how your performance is judged relative to the customer? If you're not sure what success looks like, ask.

MARCH 11

Poor customer results shouldn't set off a raging blame game of who did or didn't do what they were supposed to do. Improving customer experience is both a short- and long-term effort. Take a breath, stop the blame game, and focus on fixing customers' problems once and for all. Success in delivering awesome experience is never done and is never final.

MARCH 12

When you're dealing with an upset customer, take a moment to gather your thoughts and boost your inner reserves of patience. Don't let the customer's behavior alter yours. You are in charge of how you respond.

MARCH 13

You have two ears and one mouth. Use them in that proportion. It simply isn't possible to help a customer in distress if you don't really listen to his or her needs and concerns.

MARCH 14

Listening is not hearing. Listening is intensely focusing on the message behind the words. That means being quiet and not letting yourself be distracted by whatever else is going on around you. You can substantially improve your listening skills by repeating back to the customer what you think you heard him or her say. Practice it.

MARCH 15

If you are in a face-to-face interaction with a customer, pay close attention to what his or her body language is telling you. And be warned: Crossed arms signal defensive resistance.

MARCH 16

The best way to prevent customer interactions from spiraling out of control is to know your stuff. Obviously, you should be an expert on your part of your business. You should also work to increase your expertise in those other parts of your business with whom your customers are interacting. There is nothing worse than an employee who has even less knowledge about his or her company's products and practices than the customer does.

MARCH 17

If you want to provide awesome customer experience, you need to be proactive. You know the customer's path before he or she does. Be the one in control, managing and communicating what will happen to the customer and when.

MARCH 18

At a minimum, how you and your team are doing with regard to customer experience should be discussed every week. Every day would be better. The very best customer experience companies in the world talk about it every day, at the beginning of every shift.

MARCH 19

Do what you say you're going to do, when you said you were going to do it. There's nothing more frustrating for a customer than to be told, "Let me look into this and I will get back to you," only to never hear back from the company's representative. Follow through. Keep your word. Your promise is a commitment.

MARCH 20

Try not to let anything (physical) get between you and the customer with whom you are speaking. A desk, a kiosk, a notebook, a clipboard, or even a cup of coffee held in front of your body is often unconsciously perceived as a barrier to open communication.

MARCH 21

Real smiles work. Fake smiles don't. A real smile moves your whole face, not just your mouth. Customers subconsciously know when you're being sincere and when you're not. Look at 'em and smile. It's disarming and contagious!

MARCH 22

Interacting with customers day in and day out is tough. You're not going to be brilliant every time. Even so, you should try to be. The challenge for customer service professionals isn't to never make a mistake; it's to learn from your mistakes. When you fall down, you must get back up and try again with the next interaction.

MARCH 23

When solving customer problems, be decisive. Look and act like you know that you're offering the best possible solution to their problems. Gather all the information you can, propose a solution, and ask if it works for the customer. The more confident and deliberate you seem, the more likely your proposed solution will be accepted.

MARCH 24

It's not easy to let a barrage of negative customer behavior roll off your back like water off a duck. Sometimes, you just need to persevere. As Winston Churchill said, "If you are going through hell, keep going."

MARCH 25

For most people, listening is a skill that they must develop. It takes practice. If you can listen to learn and suspend (for a moment) your immediate desire to automatically answer, you will likely hear something deeper and more meaningful than you originally thought.

MARCH 26

Listen with generosity. Being open to what someone really needs means you have to be okay with ambiguity. Sometimes, people have a hard time making clear what they want. Be patient. Listen for their particular dream.

MARCH 27

When you open your mouth to speak to a customer, he or she will immediately decide to either agree or disagree with what you say. If the customer agrees, he or she will ask more questions, like what, when, where, and how. If the customer disagrees, he or she will either argue or mentally check out. If faced with a customer who disagrees with you, don't just keep going. Stop and start again.

MARCH 28

Look like you're paying attention by actively listening. Hear the customer's complete story before you begin formulating your response. Show that you are listening by acknowledging what the person is saying. A simple nod of the head or a "Yes, I understand" often does the trick.

MARCH 29

Your customers likely interact with your organization across dozens of different touchpoints. A *touchpoint* is simply a place where the customer and your company intersect. Touchpoints include everything from your website to your call center to your emails and texts and everything in between. Each interaction, each touchpoint, should deliver the specific customer experience intention you desire.

MARCH 30

Have you had any specific training on customer problem resolution? Do you know how to de-escalate customer interactions that have gotten out of hand? There are dozens of resources out there to build your skills. Search out some helpful tips and practice, practice, practice.

MARCH 31

Are your customers — the ones with whom you have just interacted — evangelists for your outstanding customer experience skills? After an interaction with you, your customers should want to share their positive experiences with others. You're looking for something along the line of, "You won't believe the interaction I just had with…!"

APRIL

APRIL 1

Overhead on a recent Southwest flight:

> To fasten your seat belt, insert the small metal tab into the buckle and pull on the belt to tighten. Lift up to release. It works just like every other seat belt. If you don't know how it works by now, you probably shouldn't be out in public unsupervised.

Relax. Remember that customers like to have fun, too.

APRIL 2

Customer problems only get bigger and more difficult to solve with time. Fix little problems fast, before they grow into big ones.

APRIL 3

Look busy, not rushed. A customer's confidence in your ability is determined in large part by how competent you seem. If you're rushing around, you don't look like you're in control of things. That lack of control will translate into customer worry and concern.

APRIL 4

Always be learning. Take a lesson from Jake the Dog in the cartoon series *Adventure Time*. He says, "Suckin' at something is the first step to being sorta good at something." The time you invest to improve might be painful, but the payoff will be wonderful.

APRIL 5

Experiences age well — much better than physical things. People can relive memories of awesome experiences for years to come. For example, if you chat with someone who's just come back from a vacation overseas, you'll find that they typically talk about the people they met and the experiences they had — not the things they bought.

APRIL 6

Most customers are social animals. Engaging their senses — taste, touch, sight, smell, and sound — enriches their experience. The absence of these things is called *sensory deprivation,* a commonly used torture technique. What can you do at your customer touchpoint to improve more sensory aspects of their experience?

APRIL 7

Are you afraid of talking to people you don't know? Don't be. At the beginning of an interaction, people don't pay much attention to what you say. They pay more attention to the way you say it. Don't worry about the words. Relax, and you'll communicate just fine.

APRIL 8

Customer interaction is a two-way street. When you talk, the customer is likely listening. Likewise, when the customer talks, you should listen. Beginning a conversation is like rolling a rock down a hill. You just have to get it started!

APRIL 9

When conducting a customer transaction, it's fine to ask yes-or-no questions. But if you're *really* trying to engage a customer, try asking open-ended questions. These will encourage a response that will allow the customer to open up. Here's one that works well: "What's your opinion about...?"

APRIL 10

One of the secrets of creating great customer interactions is knowing that they aren't about you. They're about the customer you're speaking with and listening to.

APRIL 11

Don't assume that all your customers are Internet or technologically savvy. After all, the World Wide Web has only been around for a little over 20 years. You likely have customers who aren't as comfortable or knowledgeable about it as you are. If you happen to run across one of these dinosaurs, slow down. Explain.

APRIL 12

You're smarter than you think you are—
and that's a problem! Because you've
had months (perhaps years) to
understand the technical ins and outs of
what you're trying to explain in
minutes, you likely speak abstractly, in
terms customers might not understand.
That means they get lost, and you get
frustrated. It's called the *curse of
knowledge*. The antidote? Slow down.
Explain with empathy. Your customers
simply don't know everything that you
do.

APRIL 13

Don't leap to answers without listening for what the customer really needs. Even though customers may sound as if they know what they want, it can't hurt to verify. A great statement to ask is, "Let me make sure I'm understanding what you're trying to get done?"

APRIL 14

Too many choices confuse customers. Try to create decision options for customers that are easily understood and simple to make. Crest (the toothpaste people) are rumored to have close to 35 different kinds of toothpaste. At what point do more choices actually become a burden?

APRIL 15

If a customer wants to learn more about a product, service, or solution you offer, how easy is it for him or her to do so? Can you work with others in your organization to provide easy-to-understand info-graphics, YouTube videos, or help guides?

APRIL 16

Customers want fast, efficient service. But more often than not, they'd like a little more than just a super-fast transaction. Your job is to do some quick detective work to see if you can add a little engagement into the mix. If the customer is all business and just wants to move on, by all means let him or her do so. Just don't assume that's what every customer wants. It's not.

APRIL 17

Customers typically have three objectives in any interaction:

- Get the transaction completed.
- Make smart decisions in the process of doing so.
- Have an interesting or engaging experience along the way.

APRIL 18

Do your customers trust your organization? Do they trust you? In the highly connected world in which we live, customers want to interact with companies and people they can trust. Customers are overwhelmed by advertising and marketing. How can you be instantly perceived as their trusted advisor?

APRIL 19

Ever had buyer's remorse — that sense of regret you sometimes get after buying a product or service? This feeling of "What did I just commit to?" stems from a fear of making a wrong or uninformed choice or an extravagant or thoughtless purchase. Customers almost always have some small sense of remorse when purchasing a product or service. What can you do or say that will help ease this natural human feeling?

APRIL 20

Sooner or later, every customer-facing employee screws up a customer interaction. When this happens to you, take a moment to learn from your mistake. It might seem strange, but you should also share your missteps with others. Doing so will help you gain some different perspectives on how the situation might have been better handled. It will also help you realize that everyone makes mistakes. Learn from your successes *and* your failures.

APRIL 21

Customers expect you to manage time well — not just yours, but theirs. In fact, you should consider the customer's time to be even more valuable than your own. This doesn't mean you need to rush. It just means you need to ensure the customer doesn't feel like you've wasted his or her time. Time is a precious commodity. Treat your customers' time like gold, and they'll be very grateful.

APRIL 22

Be ready for surprises. Adapting to whatever the customer throws your way is a sign of a true customer service professional.

APRIL 23

Providing great customer experience requires tenacity. Indeed, tenacity is the principal requirement of greatness in any work. Perhaps Chris Hadfield, the first Canadian to walk in space, put it best: "There are no wishy-washy astronauts. You don't get up there by being uncaring and blasé."

APRIL 24

If you really want to advance your skills in the customer service field, consider cracking open a book or two on human psychology. Try *The Power of Habit* by Charles Duhigg. Learning about human behavior will make it easier for you to make genuine connections with customers.

APRIL 25

As people get older, they can sometimes also slowly lose their abilities. To compensate for this, they adjust their behavior. When dealing with an older customer, you too must alter your approach and mannerisms. Speak clearly and slowly. Don't use acronyms or slang expressions. Take a little extra time to listen. Be aware that with older customers, things sometimes take a little longer. It's okay. You'll getting older too.

APRIL 26

About one in five customers in the United States have a disability. Of those, fourteen percent have difficulty seeing, thirteen percent have trouble hearing, and more than half have a hard time walking. When interacting with a person with a disability, you may need to modify your speech, behaviors, and actions accordingly. Remember, too, that just because you can't see a disability doesn't mean one isn't present.

APRIL 27

For customers with intellectual disabilities, try these tips:

- Don't presume to know what a customer can or cannot do.
- Use clear language and speak in short sentences.
- Make sure your customer understands what you've said. Don't be afraid to ask them if you have been clear in your explanation.
- Supply one piece of information at a time. Try not overload the customer with data too quickly.

APRIL 28

Every customer has five "wants":

- To be in control of what's happening
- To be treated with dignity and respect
- To be given undivided attention
- For his or her time to be respected
- A sincere apology when mistakes are made

APRIL 29

For some customer experience professionals, empathy is the first quality to go. But having empathy enables you to not only understand your customer's situation, beliefs, and ideas, but also the significance of the customer's situation and his or her emotions. Deeply listening to and truly engaging with what a customer is communicating about his or her situation is very hard work. If you have empathy, you'll more quickly gain the trust of your customers.

APRIL 30

Lessons learned from a Navy Seal:

Awareness is a choice. You have to choose to pay attention. Once you consciously make that choice, your brain takes over. Situational awareness is when you consciously decide to pay attention to everything that's going on around you and for your customers. Your ability to quickly scan a situation, its challenges, and its opportunities, while continuing to pay attention to your normal job is a skill that can be learned and improved. The thing to avoid is "focus lock" — when you're fixated on doing one thing and miss bigger cues as to what's going on around you (think tunnel vision).

MAY

MAY 1

Asking for critique is hard, but necessary. Find someone who does a better job than you do at some aspect of customer experience and ask that person to observe your interactions with customers. Then ask for his or her feedback on how you could improve. If you want to be more effective, look for people who do your job well. Copy and steal their ideas! If you ask, they won't mind.

MAY 2

Customers often have a preconceived idea of how things should work. Sometimes they're right. But often, they're wrong. As you work with customers, be aware that they may already have an idea in their head of how things are supposed to go. That means your explanations will have to achieve two things: shifting the customer's thought process away from what he or she already believes and ensuring the customer thoroughly understands and considers your new suggestion. It's a two-step dance: shift first, then sell the new idea.

MAY 3

Customers need help making decisions. Fortunately, you can act as a trusted advisor to your customers. Remember, you're an expert at what you do — far more so than your customers. Chances are, your thoughtful recommendations will be well received!

MAY 4

The following are some of the most desirable qualities in a customer-facing employee:

- Willingness to be helpful
- Kindness
- Tolerance
- Ability to follow through

As for the least desirable characteristics, they are as follows:

- Suspiciousness
- Selfishness
- Impatience
- Unpredictability

Where do you stand?

MAY 5

> When all is said and done, more is said than done.
>
> — Aesop

Customers are drowning in promises. But what they *really* want is action. That is, they want you to follow through on your promise.

After you finish talking with a customer about what you're going to do to fix his or her problem, *do it*. Don't let anything stand in the way of you completing the task. If someone other than you must complete the task, ride that person like a thoroughbred until the task finished. After the task is complete, be sure to circle back to the customer to make sure it's done to his or her satisfaction.

MAY 6

Faced with an unhappy customer? That's not surprising. Humans are feeling machines. When dealing with upset customers, there's one hard and fast rule: Don't appeal to them with logic—at least not right out of the gate. First, acknowledge their emotional state of mind. Empathize. Offer an authentic apology. After you've established an emotional connection—then and only then—you can apply logic. Remember, human behavior is seldom logical. We are driven mostly by emotion.

MAY 7

If you're dealing with a distressed customer, try asking the following question: "What would you like to have happen next?" When the customer answers, listen attentively. Then see if you can act on the customer's request. The results can be powerful!

MAY 8

Is there anything you can do to better connect your customers with each other? Can you produce webinars, customer panels, or learning workshops that will bring customers together? If you can create communities for your customers, chances are you'll learn as much as they do from the interactions that result.

MAY 9

Has anyone ever broken your trust? Maybe your brother or sister threw you under the bus. Or maybe your boss took credit for your good work. Whatever the circumstance, you no doubt discovered that once trust is broken, it's very difficult to repair. Don't do anything that breaks a customer's trust.

MAY 10

Customer experiences that deliver just a tiny bit more than the customer expects go further in creating great relationships than you might expect. The benefits of doing just a little bit extra almost always outweigh the effort of doing so.

MAY 11

No matter what happens during a customer interaction, remember that your customer is human, too. It's entirely possible that the customer you're interacting is dealing with one or more of the following:

- Concern for a loved one in the military
- Caring for a sick child
- Dealing with a lost job
- Struggling to pay bills
- Struggling with a drug or alcohol dependency

Try a little kindness.

MAY 12

What customers believe about your company is significantly influenced by what they think about you and the experience you deliver. What do you want your organization to stand for in the customer's mind? Be that.

MAY 13

Typically, most customers will have dealt with a few of your organization's employees before they get to you. Each customer's experience is formed across multiple points of interaction with your company. From their perspective, they're not coming to you individually — you're just part of an ongoing set of interactions (good or bad).

MAY 14

Do you know who your customers typically deal with *after* they interact with you? Consider asking those employees whether you inadvertently cause any customer pain that they then have to clear up.

MAY 15

It's easy to fall into the habit of using jargon and other language that your customers don't understand. After all, they probably don't have your technical knowledge. When you explain things to your customers, do their eyes glaze over? If so, it may be because you're not speaking a language that they understand.

MAY 16

While it's true that customers probably
don't have your technical knowledge,
you shouldn't think of them as
nincompoops. Don't insult customers by
acting like they're morons.

MAY 17

When explaining something to a customer, analogies work great. To come up with a good analogy, pinpoint the general idea you're trying to convey. Then find something from real life that illustrates that idea.

MAY 18

After you explain something to your customer, don't just assume he or she understood what you said. Instead, ask a simple follow-up question like, "Does that make sense?" or "Did I explain it more clearly that time?" If the answer is no, then try and try again.

MAY 19

Asking whether your customer understands something may not be enough. In that case, you should test for understanding. For example, after you explain how your product works, ask the customer to perform a task so you're sure they understand it. Most customers will appreciate the extra effort you take to ensure their complete understanding!

MAY 20

If you're ever tempted to make a negative assumption about a customer, think of Susan Boyle. She was the plain, middle-aged singer with frizzy hair and a frumpy dress who appeared a few years back on the TV show *Britain's Got Talent*.

After she walked on stage, answering a few questions from the judges revealed that she lived alone with her cat. Not only had she never been married, she had never been kissed! It was clear from the audience's reaction that they had dismissed her. But then she sang…and everything changed. Since that performance, Susan Boyle has sold more than 19 million albums worldwide, received two Grammy Award nominations, and her *Britain's Got Talent* video has been downloaded more than 100 million times.

The moral of the story? Never make assumptions about people!

MAY 21

Customers depend on their five senses to navigate and interpret the world around them. How do things look from your customer's perspective? What do things sound like? How do they smell? Taste? Feel? Can you do anything today to positively alter your customers' sensory experiences during their interactions with you or your organization?

MAY 22

Here are four simple things that you can
do today:

- Don't interrupt when your customer
  is talking.
- Say hello before the customer
  expects it.
- Listen with all of your senses
  activated.
- Say you're sorry if you have done
  something wrong.

MAY 23

Instead of asking a customer how his or her day is going, choose a question that breaks from the norm. Try asking something like, "Has anything really great happened to you yet today?" This lets your customer know you truly are interested in how he or she is doing. It's amazing how many customers will open up to a sincerely asked question!

MAY 24

It's easy to become annoyed when a customer barrages you with questions that you've answered a thousand times before. Don't. As far as customers are concerned, part of your job is to be a great teacher.

MAY 25

Be available to your customers when
you promised you would be. If you can,
open early and close late. Being
available builds trust.

MAY 26

If you have the opportunity to send a follow-up note, text, e-mail, or, better yet, handwritten note, please do. This small, simple act shows authentic care and concern.

MAY 27

You know what your customer is probably going to have to do next, right? If so, do what you can to help the customer anticipate what's coming and help him or her prepare for it. Don't let your customer think back and say, "If I had only known...." Do your best to anticipate the unexpressed needs and desires of your customers.

MAY 28

Being fair, honest, and ethical trumps everything. If you find yourself being asked to stretch the truth or otherwise act in ways that are wrong, find a different job. You deserve better, and so do your customers. If you're feeling unsure about whether what you're doing is the "right thing to do," tactfully ask. Odds are, you already know the answer.

MAY 29

As with relationships in our personal lives, relationships with customers can be short-term or long-term. To nurture a long-term relationship with a customer, make it a point to find out the customer's likes and dislikes, what makes the customer frustrated, and what his or her successes are. Then work this information into your interactions with that customer. I guarantee it will lead to stronger relationships and a better customer experience!

MAY 30

If you want to be competitive in customer experience, it's not enough to react well. Your goal is to anticipate. You can't provide excellent customer experience on autopilot.

MAY 31

Do you have any input into who is going to be hired onto your team? If so, look for people with the following characteristics (in addition, of course to the technical ability required to do the job):

- Does the person want to be of service?
- Is he or she a caring person?
- Is the person a go-getter who will take initiative in solving customer problems?
- Will the person be able to anticipate what the customer may need next?
- Is the person friendly and sociable?

If your candidate doesn't have these basic attributes, keep looking.

JUNE

JUNE 1

You must fully engage in each customer interaction. Ritz-Carlton, a leader in the delivery of consistently great experience, lays it out:

- Give a warm and sincere greeting.
- Use the customer's name during the interaction.
- Anticipate and then fulfill customer needs.
- Give a warm goodbye using the customer's name.

JUNE 2

Getting feedback from your customers is one of the best ways to improve your organization's product or service. There's nothing more valuable than the opinions of people who use your offerings every day.

If a customer offers feedback, take the time to listen, with the idea that you can use it to improve your product. Make sure you pass on any suggestions for improvements to those who can put them to work.

JUNE 3

Some chow time recommendations:

- Don't eat on the phone when you're talking to customers.
- Don't eat in front of customers in any food-service situation.
- If you're eating with a client over a meal, try to remember every table-manners lesson you've ever learned.

JUNE 4

Don't paste a smile on your face. It's fake. You know its fake. The customer knows its fake, too. When dealing with a frustrated customer, look and act appropriately concerned.

JUNE 5

Customers need to be heard. They need attention. They get cranky when they feel rushed, processed, or disrespected. When dealing with an upset customer, make sure you respond in ways that make him or her feel heard and attended to. Take care of the person first and the problem second.

JUNE 6

Want to know the customer experience golden rule? Simple. Treat others as you would like to be treated — only just a little bit better. Show authentic concern for the customer's situation.

JUNE 7

Every customer problem is unique to that person. It's probably not unique to you, however. In fact, you might have dealt with that particular issue a dozen times before. The challenge for you, then, is to not sound canned. Don't modulate your voice. Avoid sounding scripted. Instead, convey to the customer that you are concerned and genuinely interested in resolving his or her problem.

JUNE 8

Have you ever been offered a solution to a problem that had nothing whatsoever to do with the problem that you raised? Frustrating, right? To avoid making this mistake with your customers, tailor your response to each customer. The definition of *tailor* is to make or adapt something to suit a particular purpose or individual. Nothing standardized about that!

JUNE 9

More than anything, customers like, want, and need to be heard. The best way to let someone know you are listening is to repeat back what you just heard him or her say. Try this at home. I promise, your husband, wife, girlfriend, boyfriend, dog, or cat will appreciate you actually paying attention for a change!

JUNE 10

A sincere apology delivered with genuine concern is a powerful thing. But often, people think they're apologizing when really, they aren't. For example, saying "Thanks for your patience" is not an apology. Neither is saying "Wow, that took longer than I thought it would!" An apology starts with "I'm sorry" and continues with the specific thing for which you are, in fact, sorry. It's not hard. But if you really listen for those words, you'll notice how infrequently they're actually uttered.

JUNE 11

Conducting regular check-ins during conversations with customers is a great idea. In other words, think about what you've heard so far and repeat it back to the customer in your own words. Start this by saying something like, "Just to be sure I'm clear on this..." or "It sounds to me as if...."

JUNE 12

Managing conversations with customers is no easy feat. It takes practice and a little thought. If there's a lull in the conversation, try uttering little words of encouragement, like "I see" or "Hmmm." If the customer gets stuck, wait a moment to see if the silence will draw him or her out. If customer needs a little push, say something like, "Can you tell me a little more about that?" Good conversation management is a game. Play it.

JUNE 13

When dealing with customers, be sure to avoid these conversation killers:

- **Asking "why" questions:** This puts your customer on the defensive.
- **Interrupting:** Being too quick to jump in signals that you're not listening for the customer's unique perspective.
- **Lecturing:** Never use phrases like "You should have…" or "The right thing to do would have been to…."

Fortunately, there are plenty of phrases that encourage the conversation to continue:

- "Excuse me…."
- "May I ask a clarifying question?"
- "Maybe we could start by…."

JUNE 14

If you're faced with a customer who is truly angry, don't tell him or her to "calm down." That's like pouring gasoline on a fire. Let the person vent his or her anger or frustration uninterrupted. Don't talk. Convey that you're paying attention by nodding your head and use facial expressions to show your concern. Nine out of ten times, after people have had a chance to fully express their anger, they will be willing to work with you to find a solution. The key for you is to be quiet and let the person vent. No interrupting. No judgment. No excuses. Just listen.

JUNE 15

It's hard not to take things personally. But the best customer-service professionals understand they must never give customers the power to push their buttons and control their feelings. Sure, a rude customer can mess with your emotions for a few minutes. But don't allow a customer's behavior to affect your sense of who you are. Instead, take a deep breath. Create some distance between you and your reactions. Don't take the insult personally. After all, the customer doesn't really know you. Most importantly, remember that you are in charge of this interaction.

JUNE 16

Need a great comeback after being verbally attacked by a customer? This one allows you to both stay in control *and* be perceived as very reasonable in the process: "You seem angry, frustrated, or at the very least really upset with me personally. Can you tell me what I can do that will be good solution for both of us? If you want to continue to be angry, that's fine. But I really would like to solve this problem for you." It's disarming in a very nice way.

JUNE 17

Sadly, in our culture, we don't honor our senior citizens. Ageism is as prevalent as racism, sexism, and lots of other "isms." But you can help change that. When you interact with an older customer, take the time to treat them as individuals worthy of your attention rather than as "a cranky old man" or an "old granny" who has "nothing better to do than take up your time."

JUNE 18

In your conversations with customers, listen for their pain, joy, successes, and fears. These will always be present, whether visibly or under the surface. When your customers understand that you are listening to them with that degree of intensity, they will work with you to solve problems and, ultimately, buy more of what you (or your organization) are selling.

JUNE 19

Don't be afraid to make mistakes with customers. It's not the end of the world. Nobody's perfect. When you do screw up, talk to your team about it. That way, you can all learn from your mistake. What did you screw up yesterday?

JUNE 20

When it comes to interacting with customers, how's your stamina? Are you pooped out by lunchtime? Or can you make until the end of the day? Consistently delivering exceptional customer experience is more a marathon than a sprint. You have to hang in there until it's over. That being said, take breaks if you can, and plan for setbacks during the day or week. Most importantly, think positively. Nothing builds mental resilience like self-confidence!

JUNE 21

Feel like you're all alone in your quest to improve customer experience? You probably aren't, but it sure can seem that way sometimes. Try to find other employees who share your interest in delivering better service. Don't just look for these like-minded colleagues at your customer touchpoint; look upstream and downstream in your organization as well.

JUNE 22

What is your supervisor's mindset when it comes to improving customer service? There's a decent chance he or she might not "get it." It may take a while to get bosses who've been around awhile heading in the right direction. If they really don't care and the organization isn't going to force them to, then do your best to deliver the very best personal customer experience you can. It will pay off eventually.

JUNE 23

Remember the kid's game *Chutes and Ladders*? Whether you won or lost depended entirely on random luck. Playing the game required no skill whatsoever. As a player, you had no real control over the outcome.

While that's fine for very young kids, adults expect a little more control — which explains why customers don't like it when they have no control over what is happening to them. Is there anything you can do to give your customers more control — or, at a minimum, the illusion of control?

JUNE 24

Your customer's experience is created across all the points of interaction that he or she has with your organization. Today, you have the customer for a little while, but that customer is on a long journey with your organization. What will he or she remember about your particular part of the trip?

JUNE 25

Does your organization have internal service standards that pertain to how and when you and your team provide service to other internal departments or employees? If so, ask yourself these four questions:

- Do I know who my internal customers are?
- How am I doing at delivering what my internal customers expect from me?
- How do I know how I'm doing?
- When was the last time I sat down and talked to my internal customers about what they might need (or not need) from me?

JUNE 26

Job shadowing (sometimes called *ride-a-longs*) allows a person from one department to spend time with an employee from another. Try it. I promise you'll discover more than you ever imagined about what other parts of your organization struggle with in delivering better customer experience. Find out if your organization does ride-a-longs. If not, volunteer to be the first.

JUNE 27

Is a fellow team member resisting your (or your organization's) efforts to improve customer experience? That's no surprise. No one likes change. When faced with doing something new, most employees may ask one or all of the following questions:

- What's in it for me?
- What can I do with it?
- How will this change my job?
- Is it really possible to do?
- If I don't do it, will anything bad happen to me?

Is there anything you can do to help your fellow employees get the answers to these questions?

JUNE 28

Great customer experience does not start with the customer. It starts with the people who *work* with the customer. Be very picky about who you select to work with customers. Don't just hire people who have the technical skills for the job without thinking about whether they can deliver the customer experience you want. Hire people with *all* the skills you need.

JUNE 29

Great customer experience is an outcome. More often than not, customer experience is based on the interplay between engaged employees, internal processes that work well, and customers who sense whether an organization truly cares.

JUNE 30

Today, customers can provide feedback on your service experience in dozens of ways:

- In person
- Through a text
- By snail mail
- Via e-mail
- By posting comments and videos on social media
- On the phone
- By filling in a survey
- By leaving a comment on your Web site

Are you and your organization listening at all of the places where your customers are talking?

JULY

JULY 1

Although technology can help provide more intimate experiences for customers, it is rarely a complete solution in its own right. Yes, technology can help you remember details about customer interactions, but it doesn't do a very good job with the softer skills of interpersonal communications. That's your job. Don't let the machine control or stand in the way of great experience. You do it. You're much better at it.

JULY 2

Does your performance — and that of your team — consistently exceed your customers' expectations? If not, why? Pick one thing to do differently *today*.

JULY 3

What three words would your most recent customer use to describe his or her interaction with you? No lying or exaggerating. Are you okay with that answer?

JULY 4

In an 1803 letter, Thomas Jefferson wrote: "Some men (and women) are born for public service". Is this you?

JULY 5

In the old days (15 years ago), a dissatisfied customer might on average, tell seven friends and acquaintances about his or her bad experience. Today, thanks to social media, dissatisfied customers tell approximately 20 people on average what went wrong. If there is an upset customer anywhere in your vicinity, you need to do everything possible to fix that person's problem. Don't let him or her start venting elsewhere!

JULY 6

Companies invest millions of dollars in marketing campaigns to attract new customers — but spend almost nothing to *keep* them. This makes zero sense. Retaining customers by delivering a great experience is a lot more economical than finding new customers to replace ones who leave due to a poor experience. New bumper sticker idea: "Save our customers!"

JULY 7

Most customers leave without saying a word. Poof! They're gone. It's not that they wouldn't be happy to share their observations and concerns about their experience. It's that often, nobody asks. If you have reason to think a customer isn't completely happy — any reason at all — ask. Then get busy fixing what's wrong.

JULY 8

Don't be afraid to ask your customer the difficult question, "Are you happy with us?" If the customer knows you're sincere and really want the feedback — and that you'll act immediately on his or her input — then he or she will gladly tell you everything you need to know.

JULY 9

Have you ever run into a friendly but clueless service person? Sure, they're nice, but they can't help you solve your problem. Look, if you can't deliver the basics, it doesn't matter how delightful and engaging your personality is. Your customers are going to leave frustrated. Make sure you can deliver on *all* the basic requirements first. Your customers expect that. Then move on to delivering delight.

JULY 10

Your customer's experience with your organization spans many different points of interaction. Your job is not just to smooth out your individual section of the track they're traveling, but to fix any rough patches immediately before and after your touchpoint.

JULY 11

Changing customer experience doesn't require a radical, top-to-bottom makeover of every aspect of your organization. Most organizations, like most people, do better when change happens on a smaller scale. What is one very small change you can make today for your customers?

JULY 12

You've probably heard the expression "Put yourself in the customer's shoes." But what does that mean? It means having empathy. When it comes to delivering great customer experience, having empathy is job #1. To *empathize* means to focus on someone else's emotional state. To do this effectively, you first have to stop thinking about yourself.

JULY 13

When a customer is about to explode with anger, it's time for you to do the opposite. If the customer raises his or her voice, lower yours. If the customer is talking super fast, slow your pace down just a little. You might find that this will help prevent the situation from spiraling out of control.

JULY 14

Do you play golf? More importantly, do you play it *well*? Most people don't. It's a tough mental sport. Too many people study the discipline forever, memorizing the right steps, learning the right actions, and breaking things down into smaller and smaller technical elements — only to lose all sense of perspective. Sooner or later, you have to trust yourself, trust what you've learned, and just go *do* it. The same goes for delivering great customer experience. It's a game. Play it. Enjoy it. And keep score.

JULY 15

The great productivity guru David Allen has a two-minute rule that applies well to customer-facing professionals: "If an action will take less than two minutes, that action should be taken in that immediate moment." Fix little problems now. Unattended little problems turn into big ones. They get harder to solve and more expensive over time.

JULY 16

Creating great customer experience means always seeking to be perfect — but knowing that you're often going to fail in the pursuit. Learn from your mistakes. There is no perfection — there is only the pursuit of it.

JULY 17

In our very busy digital world, getting and keeping a customer's attention can mean the difference between success and failure. Maintaining a customer's attention is the secret of productive and engaging experiences. In what way are your customer interactions captivating?

JULY 18

A chameleon changes its color and texture depending upon its environment. Highly adaptable, chameleons thrive by blending in. In your interactions with customers, you'll need to do the same. You'll need to be relatable, to instantly identify with how the customer perceives his or her world. In this way, you can build quick acceptance and trust with them.

JULY 19

Human beings have a limited attention span. The human brain always looks for shortcuts to understand things and make decisions. Long, convoluted explanations don't cut it. When interacting with customers, be simple, precise, and to the point. Get them the information they need as quickly and clearly as you can.

JULY 20

These days, it seems like it's all about standardizing processes to make them lean and efficient. But although scripts and standards are important, so is personalized (read: human) interaction. Can you go off-script with your customers, staying true to the intention of the script but allowing some of your personality to come through?

JULY 21

Simple is better than complex. Always. What can you do to simplify things for the customer? Start by removing everything from your explanations, messages, services, or offerings that isn't absolutely critical.

JULY 22

When dealing with a customer, ask yourself these six questions:

- What is the situation?
- What is the problem or concern I hope to fix?
- What does the customer want?
- What does your organization need or want out of this interaction?
- How do I want the customer to feel?
- How can I make that happen?

JULY 23

Effective customer communication is never just you talking or just them talking. It's two-way. It's interactive. There must be a feedback loop to ensure understanding by all parties involved. Remember, it is your responsibility to lead and manage the discussion.

JULY 24

Organizations expend considerable effort to break their customers down into defined segments based on typical behaviors and motivations. That's all fine for sales and marketing people to target a particular audience for acquisition. But it doesn't work so well for those working with individual customers. A customer's attitude, perspective, and behavior are not static. Customers are fluid, independent creatures whose point of view can and will change on the fly. Carefully listen for each individual customer's story, issue, or concerns in that moment.

JULY 25

Your customers have hopes, dreams, and aspirations — not just for their lives as a whole, but for each day and even for each specific interaction. Do you know what their hopes are for their interaction with you?

JULY 26

You spent much of your youth learning to speak, read, and write. But how much training and education have you had on how to *listen*? Probably not much. Is it time for you to learn how to listen better?

JULY 27

When it comes to communication, many customer service professionals focus on being understood — clearly stating their point, their organization's polices, or whatever else they want to convey. But chances are that while you're busy explaining, your customer isn't really listening. Why? Because you haven't taken the time to understand their position first. As noted by the great Steven Covey in *The 7 Habits of Highly Effective People*, we ought to "seek first to understand, and then to be understood."

JULY 28

In any customer interaction, start where the customer is. Meet them wherever they are, not where you're coming from.

JULY 29

If you tell a customer that you're going to take action on something, do it — *now*. Not following up on promises is the fastest way to destroy your relationship.

JULY 30

Connecting with customers has as much to do with touching their hearts and emotions as it does with logic, facts, and reason. Of course, you need to have full command of details and specifications. But to be *really* successful at engaging customers, you must connect with them personally and emotionally.

JULY 31

At the beginning of your next customer interaction, ask yourself these two questions:

- What matters most to the customer right now?
- How can I address those concerns?

AUGUST

AUGUST 1

Henry Ford once said, "If there is any one secret of success, it lies in the ability to get the other person's point of view and see things from that person's angle as well as your own." In the spirit of Henry Ford, reverse roles with one of your customers today. Put yourself completely in his or her place.

AUGUST 2

You're probably familiar with the Golden Rule. It states that you should treat others as you would like others to treat you. The reverse of this is also true: Don't treat others in way that you would not like to be treated.

AUGUST 3

People learn by doing. But just doing isn't enough. You also need to examine your results to see whether you are getting the outcomes you want. Take a moment during each day to reflect on what's working and what isn't. Then, if you need to, make changes.

Do. Reflect. Modify if necessary. Repeat.

AUGUST 4

Here are four questions to ask yourself (and maybe your manager):

- What do you personally need to do to improve your interaction with customers?
- How are you supposed to get better?
- Why do you want to keep improving?
- When are you supposed to get better?

If you don't know the answers to these questions, then go find out.

AUGUST 5

Many customers will agree to your proposed solutions if they perceive them as acceptable to a majority of other people — something called *social proof*. This explains why close to 90 percent of consumers read online reviews when considering purchasing a product or service. Try to weave the idea of social proof into your next conversation with a customer conversation.

AUGUST 6

When you engage in a dialogue with a customer, you establish your trustworthiness. You must be the instigator and manager of this most important human-to-human connection.

AUGUST 7

If you offer something of value for free, customers will feel a real sense of indebtedness toward you. When customers feel this way, they are much more likely to try to return the favor the next time you request something from them.

Don't think you have anything of value that you can give away for free? Think again. Your advice, technical expertise, knowledge, and personal perspective are enormously valuable. Give them away—and don't be afraid to ask for something in return.

AUGUST 8

Asking questions enables you to lead, control, and manage conversations. But the questions have to be good ones. Customer-service rookies often stick with logical, fact-finding questions. This is a mistake. Yes, you should start by determining the facts. But you should ask authentic, emotion-based questions as well. Here are some examples:

- What is most important to you?
- What was your reaction when that happened?

AUGUST 9

It's worth repeating that one of the most powerful things you can say is your customer's first name. A person's name is a big part of who he or she is. When people are kids, they hear their name over and over again. They link hearing their name with attention and pleasure. When you say a customer's name, you acknowledge that person's identity and boost his or her self-worth.

AUGUST 10

While you should say your customer's name, don't overdo it. It's annoying. Recently, I visited my doctor for my annual checkup. He had never had much of a bedside manner. In fact, in the past, I could barely get him to look me in the eye. But he must have attended some type of seminar on connecting with his patients, because this time, he got really carried away using my name. "Now Mr. Barnes, how are we feeling today Mr. Barnes?" "Mr. Barnes, have you been taking aspirin once a day as we discussed, Mr. Barnes?" It was so irritating! After five minutes, I felt like his overuse of my name was going to give me a heart attack.

AUGUST 11

Are you big? Tall? Otherwise physically imposing? If so, be aware that many customers will be subconsciously affected by your size. People tend to be cautious around someone who is significantly bigger or taller than they are.

The opposite is also true: People tend to be less wary around someone who is smaller. If you work in customer service, you may find that there are benefits to being petite. Customers may view you as less of a threat, and may challenge you less.

AUGUST 12

Nowadays, most people live in culturally diverse communities. For this reason, it's worth studying various cultural norms. For example, to Americans, a "thumbs-up" sign is positive. But in southern Europe and some Middle Eastern countries, it is an insult. In some Arab cultures, looking someone of the opposite sex directly in the eye is seen as aggressively flirtatious. On the other hand, Southern Europeans may gaze at you for such a long time, it'll make *you* feel uncomfortable. Not everyone is the same and no one is just like you. Read up on different cultural norms so you don't stumble in your interactions.

AUGUST 13

Saying "please" and "thank you" will go a long way toward building and maintaining strong customer relationships. Good manners make you seem grateful, empathetic, and kind. When someone does something nice for you, reciprocate with words of gratitude:

- "Please, let me see how I can help you."
- "Thank you for explaining that to me."

AUGUST 14

When communicating with others, visual cues are extremely important — even more so than words. Research by UCLA professor Dr. Albert Mehrabian showed that the words spoken drive only seven percent of the listener's feelings and attitudes about the message. In contrast, the *way* the words are spoken drives thirty-eight percent of the listener's experience. And the speaker's facial expression? That accounts for fifty-five percent of the listener's experience. Don't just think about what you want to say — think about how you want to say it!

AUGUST 15

When your interaction with a customer is over, take a moment to offer a warm goodbye. Be sure to use the customer's name one last time. Last impressions last!

AUGUST 16

Anticipatory customer service isn't about doing the basics. It's way beyond just providing an acceptable transaction. It's about anticipating what the customer will need and delivering it at precisely the right moment.

AUGUST 17

What is your single objective for all of your customer interactions today? How do you want your customers to feel after their interaction with you? Once you have your answer, write it down. Be intentional about what you want to be remembered for!

AUGUST 18

Customers don't just buy products and services for what those products or services provide. They also buy them for the state of mind they reach when they use or experience the product or service. Think of it this way: People don't remember the specific rides at Walt Disney World. Rather, they remember how they felt as they experienced the park—how clean it was, how friendly the staff was, and so on.

AUGUST 19

Remember to ask yourself these three questions about the customer you're about to deal with:

- What are this customer's hopes, aspirations, and desires?
- What are their fears, concerns, and worries?
- What are you going to do to address these?

AUGUST 20

Don't start a customer interaction blind. Do a quick customer assessment before every interaction. If possible, find out the following information before you start:

- What was the customer's last interaction with your organization? Read any relevant call or interaction logs to find out.
- What is the customer's purchase or usage history?
- How does the customer perceive the quality of his or her relationship with your company?
- How did the customer respond to his or her last customer satisfaction or engagement survey?
- What has changed since the customer's last interaction with you?

AUGUST 21

Work to understand customers on their terms. Don't assume they think as you do, make decisions as you would, or share your same goals, values, and objectives. Be ready to adapt your approach as you learn more about your customer. This takes discipline and quick thinking, but it will pay off!

AUGUST 22

Most customers don't care about the inner workings of your organization. If you are unable to deliver great customer service because of some flawed internal process or other internal problem, keep it to yourself. The customer neither needs nor wants to hear about it. Fix the problem without involving the customer.

AUGUST 23

Working effectively with a customer
means quickly transitioning between:
- Presenting facts, data, and logical
  reasons
- Connecting with the customer's
  emotional state of mind
- Bringing passion and energy to
  every interaction

AUGUST 24

When you make a promise to a customer about when something will be fixed, taken care of, or looked into, speak truthfully. When it comes to estimates, don't guess, and don't just say something that sounds good in the moment. If you give a specific time, be certain you can deliver accordingly. Under promise, over deliver.

AUGUST 25

Get the answer to your customer's question as quickly as possible. The same goes for fixing problems and addressing issues. Speed wins.

AUGUST 26

Small delays in solving a customer's problem can have a much greater impact than you might think. The amount of time that passes before a problem is resolved has a disproportionate impact on the customer's belief in your sincerity and competence. Be quick.

AUGUST 27

Has something gone wrong for a customer? Step up and personally own the solution. Don't pass the buck. Make sure the customer knows that resolving his or her problem is your top priority.

AUGUST 28

Everyone is busy, but you can always find a moment to smile.

AUGUST 29

Take risks with customers. Try new things. If things go wrong, build on your mistakes. Use them as a ladder to continue climbing. Whatever you do, keep improving.

AUGUST 30

These days, customers are bombarded with choices, features, and options — but what they want is for things to be easier, simpler, and quicker. What can you do today to simplify things for your customers? How can you provide a clearer, quicker path for your customer to follow?

AUGUST 31

People often think that by providing lots of choices, they're somehow doing their customers a big favor. But too many choices is a bad thing. Give customers one or two excellent alternatives and then provide expert guidance to help them choose. Your customers will love you for it!

SEPTEMBER

SEPTEMBER 1

How many steps do your customers have to take to finish a task you're asking them to complete? Is every step really absolutely necessary? Is there anything you could eliminate to speed things up? Is there information that you already know that could be pre-filled on a form? Make it a point to reduce, reduce, and reduce some more the amount of time it takes for a customer to do anything.

SEPTEMBER 2

There is a bit of theater in every face-to-face customer interaction. Like it or not, if you're with customers, you're on stage. Being efficient and effective is great. Just don't forget that you need to be entertaining as well. Tap into the drama, laughter, and human-ness in every customer interaction.

SEPTEMBER 3

Want the best advice ever for a customer-service employee? It's this: *Make yourself useful.* Be the go-to person whenever a customer needs help. Be confident, share what you know, and give freely of your time, perspective, and expertise.

SEPTEMBER 4

Teach, don't tell. Yes, it may be easier to just solve a problem rather than tell someone else how to solve it himself or herself. But if it is likely the customer is going to encounter this problem again, teach him or her how to avoid or resolve the issue.

SEPTEMBER 5

Look for ways to give your customers more control in their interactions with you and your organization. Here are some things to consider:

- If the customer were in control, how might he or she want to complete this task?

- If the customer were in control, when would he or she like to do this task?

- If the customer were in control, where would he or she like to do this task?

Can you modify what you do to allow your customers more control?

SEPTEMBER 6

Some organizations make it very difficult for customers to rapidly resolve escalated complaints. But if there is ever a time to eliminate roadblocks for a customer, it is when things have already gone wrong. Don't let a simple problem compound. Get a handle on your organization's problem-escalation processes and see if they work in the real world.

SEPTEMBER 7

You know more about your organization's products, services, processes, and procedures than your customers ever will. When you share your knowledge in a sincere and helpful way, your customers will engage with you at a personal level. It's hard to resist advice from an insider. You're the insider here! Don' be shy. Advise.

SEPTEMBER 8

Give your customer a clear way out of his or her situation or problem. Communicate the customer's options to cancel a transaction, return a product, modify a service, or get a credit in the simplest possible terms. Don't make the customer work for a solution. Make it as easy and seamless as possible to fix a problem.

SEPTEMBER 9

Are your organization's policies and procedures designed to help customers? Or are they meant to protect the organization? Is there a way for them to do both? If you want to earn and maintain your customers' respect and trust, you must have protocols and practices that look out for their best interests.

SEPTEMBER 10

The critical factor in delivering awesome customer experience is the attitude you bring. Let customers know they are important, keep your promises, be authentic, and be caring. Simple.

SEPTEMBER 11

Sometimes, building and strengthening customer relationships happens naturally. More often than not, however, you have to work at it. To develop this skill, keep these points in mind:

- **Expectations:** Be clear about the details.
- **Openness:** Communicate clearly and honestly.
- **Caring:** Show your concern for the customer's well-being.
- **Positivity:** Stay positive. Everything can be fixed!
- **Effort:** Put in the work to manage the relationship.

SEPTEMBER 12

Avoid excessive multi-tasking while interacting with a customer. When you spread your attention over a variety of things, the customer feels left out.

SEPTEMBER 13

Everyone craves attention, and customers are no exception. Listen with all of your being. Ignore distractions. Lean forward. Act as if you are interested in hearing more. Be patient in your listening. Don't rush the customer. Nod your head to let the customer know you are really hearing what he or she is saying.

SEPTEMBER 14

My mom's purse contained everything she might conceivably need during the course of a day: Band-Aids, gum, needle and thread, Super Glue, snacks — you name it. Take a lesson from Mom and keep with you everything you will need to solve ninety-nine percent of customer problems that arise. This might be information, tools, forms, replacements, whatever. Don't scramble around for stuff you know you're going to need. Be prepared!

SEPTEMBER 15

Suppose the thing your customer wants isn't available for a couple days. You could communicate that to the customer by saying, "I can't get that for you. It's unavailable. Other than ordering it, there's nothing I can do right now." Or, you could say, "That will be available in two days. I can put the request in now and we will be sure to get it to you as soon as it is available." Both phrases communicate the same information. If you were the customer, which would you rather hear?

SEPTEMBER 16

First-contact resolution should be your goal. If you can, deal with all customer issues, complaints, and suggestions at the first point of interaction. Never pass the buck if you can help it.

SEPTEMBER 17

Help customers help themselves. Design self-service processes with care. When done right, these processes can be personal, efficient, and engaging. Make sure your processes are up to snuff by seeing for yourself what it's really like for customers to try to use them.

SEPTEMBER 18

Want to be smarter than the boss? Remember this fact: Retaining existing customers is more important, more cost-effective, and easier than finding new ones. Incredibly, even some of the smartest CEOs, marketing VPs, and other bigwigs don't grasp this simple truth. Keep the customers you have by delivering an engaging experience at every opportunity.

SEPTEMBER 19

Say thank you. The power of that simple phrase is completely underrated!

SEPTEMBER 20

Be your customers' advocate. When you see pain points in your customers' experience, talk about them — often. Make everyone in your organization aware of the problems that customers face. Be specific about issues, concerns, and challenges.

SEPTEMBER 21

Do you and members of your team deal with the same customer issues over and over again? Create a cheat sheet with best practices on how best to address and resolve common issues and what to say to customers who have them. There is no point in you or anyone else reinventing the wheel for every call or interaction.

SEPTEMBER 22

Do you have any influence on who gets hired for a customer-service job on your team? If not, can you get some influence? Ask to be part of the hiring team to screen out truly nasty candidates *before* they get hired.

SEPTEMBER 23

Believe it or not, there are some customers who you should just get rid of. These are the ones who take up your organization's time, ask for discounts, demand free stuff, or are otherwise unprofitable. When you identify these customers, flag them for your manager or supervisor. Hopefully, he or she will go ahead and fire them! Let your competitors deal with them.

SEPTEMBER 24

Vince Lombardi, the legendary coach of the Green Bay Packers, believed in preparation. According to Lombardi, when you dedicate yourself and take preparation seriously, actually playing the game is the easy part. In your daily work, you should prepare for customer interactions. Identify the possible courses of action you might take with a customer before you engage with him or her.

SEPTEMBER 25

Most people have an innate desire to improve. This stems from humankind's early days, when we lived in tribes and wanted to secure our spot as productive members of the community. But it's almost impossible to improve if you don't measure your progress over time. Track your progress in delivering better customer service on a daily or weekly basis.

SEPTEMBER 26

As writer Elbert Hubbard once said, "To avoid criticism, do nothing, say nothing, and be nothing." When it comes to improving customer service in your organization, do what you think is right—even if others criticize you for it.

SEPTEMBER 27

Most people fixate on poor performance and other negative stuff. They rarely focus on the positive things they accomplish. Give yourself a break. Think about times when you've delivered great service. Take a minute or two to recognize that you're doing great things!

SEPTEMBER 28

Examine your customer-engagement goals—at a personal or organizational level—and identify the skills you'll need to accomplish them. Then figure out how to acquire those skills.

SEPTEMBER 29

No one is perfect all the time. One person having a not-so-great day can send ripples through an entire organization, quietly affecting everyone's mood. Great people (and for that matter, great organizations) find ways to bounce back quickly, absorb mediocre performance, and rapidly remake themselves to be better than before.

SEPTEMBER 30

When you engage with customers—
when you take the time to really do it
right—something special happens. We
infuse the service we deliver with little
pieces of us. Make no mistake: Great
customer service is an act of creation.
We take our skills, our attitudes, and
our tools and breathe life into an
interaction. Maybe the interaction isn't
perfect every time. But our attempts to
be better evoke something we all crave:
the wonderful pride of craftsmanship.

OCTOBER

OCTOBER 1

When faced with a negative customer situation, don't discuss why something happened, what went wrong, or what it might cost to fix it. Instead, flip the conversation. Focus on what you can do right away to correct the situation. This tactic will deflate the customer's anger and frustration and reassure the customer that you will take care of him or her — and quickly.

OCTOBER 2

Customers can sense when you are being honest, sincere, and authentic. When you project these characteristics, you build trust. If you fail to do this, there's a good chance your customers will develop a defensive, "what will this person do to me" attitude.

OCTOBER 3

Here's your assignment for today: Write a personal note of thanks to one or more of your customers, whether they're external or internal. Be as specific as possible. Doug Conant, the former CEO of Campbell's Soup, sent more than 30,000 handwritten notes to his team during his time as the boss. The power of this simple act is both personal and lasting.

OCTOBER 4

Never look at your smart phone or tablet when you are with a customer — *unless* you need to use the device to address that particular customer's issue. If this is the case, explain exactly why you are using your device and how it will help the customer.

OCTOBER 5

If you and your organization could never find another customer, would you treat the ones you already have differently? Too often, we act as if there were an infinite supply of new customers. There isn't. Love the ones you have and don't ever lose them.

OCTOBER 6

My mom used to tell me that if I ever found myself having failed to speak the complete truth, the only way to restore trust was to own up to that fact as quickly as possible. This maxim applies to your communications with customers, too. If you find yourself in this situation with a customer, say something like this: "I'm sorry. What I originally communicated is not actually how things work. I'd like to correct my mistake."

OCTOBER 7

The very best way to communicate negative, disappointing, or otherwise bad news to a customer is to tell the plain truth. Speak the facts, and do it promptly.

OCTOBER 8

Are you exhausted by your customer interactions? Take a break and do something physical. Depending upon your work environment, you can stand, stretch, or ask a co-worker or team member to cover you for a minute or two so you can take a quick walk. Better to take a 10-second breather now than to upset a customer later!

OCTOBER 9

Albert Einstein said, "Insanity is doing the same thing over and over again and expecting different results." If whatever you're doing with your customers isn't going over so well, try something different. Ask yourself, "What could I do with my customers today that would surprise them and enable me to connect with them as human beings?"

OCTOBER 10

Today you have a choice: Do the bare minimum or go beyond what's required. Which will you choose?

OCTOBER 11

To be an awesome customer experience advocate, you have to take a stand. Make your opinions known. Draw your line in the sand about customer service and let people know it's important to you. You must declare that you're going to be different in the face of apathy.

OCTOBER 12

Do people believe what you say?
Believability can't be faked. You foster
believability by establishing trust. And
trust is simply a reflection of your
customer's experience with you over
time. Always work to establish trust.
Every second matters.

OCTOBER 13

Do the hard customer stuff yourself.
Don't delegate. Don't pass the buck. No
shirking! Own it.

OCTOBER 14

Psychologist Rollo May once said, "The opposite of courage in our society is not cowardice, it is conformity." If you want to be *really* great at delivering awesome customer service, you cannot conform. Conforming is easy. Being excellent is hard. To be excellent, you must constantly ask, "Is there a better way?"

OCTOBER 15

The biggest mistake people make is to believe they work for someone other than the customer. Don't make this mistake. Your *real* boss — the customer — should be the driving force behind everything you do.

OCTOBER 16

Carefully scripted customer service interactions often become monotonous and boring for everyone involved — you *and* the customer. Authentic customer conversations, on the other hand, are dynamic. They move and shift, intertwining facts and emotions. Work to engage your customers, not to kill them with fake dialogue!

OCTOBER 17

If you deliver great customer experience today, you will save yourself a lot of unnecessary pain and frustration tomorrow. Doing it right the first time virtually eliminates your chances of becoming embroiled in a nasty customer firefight later. When you consistently deliver great service, you keep angry customers calm by preventing them from getting ramped up in the first place or adding fuel to their already-burning bonfire of emotions.

OCTOBER 18

Drinking lots of caffeine (think soda, coffee, and energy shots) releases adrenaline. Adrenaline is the evolutionary enabler of the "fight or flight" response. This emotional response bypasses logical reasoning and puts you in an act-now state of mind. That's fantastic if you need to outrun a charging rhino. It's not so great when you interact with customers. If you find you're a little snappy with customers, lay off the caffeine shots and drink a little water.

OCTOBER 19

Do you know who to call if a customer has a question that you can't answer? Print out a card with all the phone numbers (cell phones are best) that you or your customer can use to get answers fast. Keep it in your pocket, wallet, or purse so you'll know where to find it when you need it.

OCTOBER 20

Delivering great customer service is a performance — and it's as demanding as being on stage doing five shows a day. If you do it right, you should feel emotionally and physically drained at the end of your show.

OCTOBER 21

Being a leader in customer experience isn't just about being able to do the technical aspects of the job. It's about how well you can do the technical tasks while engaging the emotions of your customer. It's not enough to do one or the other. You must do both.

OCTOBER 22

Think about the first few seconds and the last few minutes of each customer interaction. That's what your customers are going to remember. What will they remember about you?

OCTOBER 23

Complaints are great gifts — albeit wrapped in ugly packaging. Just as you would thank a customer for a compliment, thank that person for his or her complaint. Why? Because the complaint is worth more to you and your business. After all, if you know what your customer's problem is, you can fix it.

OCTOBER 24

Is a customer walking directly toward you? Don't turn away, look at your computer, pick up the phone, walk away, or do anything else that suggests that your purpose in life is anything other than to answer that person's question, meet his or her needs, or solve his or her problem.

OCTOBER 25

Has this ever happened to you? You walk up to the counter and the service person behind the desk is talking, rolling his eyes, or shaking his head about the customer he dealt with before you. It makes you wonder what that person is going to say about you when you leave! If you work in customer service, you must keep your last interaction to yourself. View every new interaction as a clean slate.

OCTOBER 26

Take a look at how your customer interactions are measured. If they are all time or speed-based (talk time, time to complete, etc.), try looking at some different kinds of measures. Focusing only on time- or speed-based measures can result in customer interactions that are abrupt or incomplete.

OCTOBER 27

Do you have any responsibility for new-hire orientation? If you're the person who on-boards new employees, make sure you teach the customer engagement side of the job as well as the technical nuts and bolts.

OCTOBER 28

Research shows that customers who are fully engaged with your organization spend more money, are more likely to forgive you when you screw up, and cost less to service. In other words, great customer service = more money!

OCTOBER 29

Here are five things to do today:

- Greet you customers by name. If you don't know a customer's name, ask.
- Anticipate. Be proactive. Approach customers before they approach you.
- Know your stuff and answer questions with confidence.
- Tailor your service to the individual. Adapt as needed to be more human.
- Be safe. That means take care personally, take care of the privacy of your customers' data, and take care as you carry out the technical aspects of your job.

OCTOBER 30

Customers don't like surprises—especially when they're in the form of fees or legal mumbo-jumbo. When conveying this type of information to customer, be as transparent as you possibly can be. Inform them of what they need to know. Just don't get bogged down. Customers just want to get their specific, immediate task accomplished.

OCTOBER 31

Customer service is not just a department. Nor is it just how you deal with complaining customers. Customer service should be in everything you do. It is a state of mind. It is your job.

NOVEMBER

NOVEMBER 1

Need to explain something complicated to a customer? Use visuals. Create graphics, drawings, and models that allow the customer to see what you're talking about. Visuals don't need to be overdone. They just need to be clear.

NOVEMBER 2

Customers absorb information at different rates of speed. Be careful not to overload, overwhelm, or otherwise overpower your them with too much information at once. Talk a little, take a moment to let them process what you're saying, and then move to the next idea, concept, or direction. Give the customer time to let your message soak in.

NOVEMBER 3

If you must talk to a group of customers at the same time, speak to them as individuals. During your conversation, shift your gaze from one customer to another. You'll know you've effectively personalized the group conversation when you see the customer you're talking to at the moment nod his or her head or perform some other action to acknowledge what you're saying.

NOVEMBER 4

Take your customers for a test drive.
What's their mood? What's their
emotional state? Can you get them take
a relaxed breath? Can you make them
laugh? Can you amaze them with your
care and compassion? Can you finish
the task more quickly than they
dreamed possible? The essence of
delivering great customer experience is
shifting the emotional state of your
customers in positive ways. Remember:
You're in the driver's seat.

NOVEMBER 5

Do you know how to receive a compliment? Here's how to take accept an accolade:

- **Smile:** A smile acknowledges the person's kind words.
- **Return the compliment:** Say something like, "It's kind of you to say that."
- **Move on quickly:** Don't let there be an awkward silence.

Simple, right? Now, go get some compliments and practice!

NOVEMBER 6

Brevity is good. Be quick. Use as few words as possible. No rambling. At the same time, balance that with being human. Personalize when possible to engage the customer. It's not easy, but that's why you're paid the big bucks.

NOVEMBER 7

Listening and maintaining eye contact go hand in hand. If you look away when a customer is explaining something, it appears as though you don't care. This is the fastest way to lose trust. Be open and display an appropriate facial expression as you listen. If you must take notes on what the customer is saying, listen first and take notes after.

NOVEMBER 8

When you a have fair amount of relevant experience, trust your instincts during your interactions with customer. Your intuition will become even better the longer you're in a job or a role.

NOVEMBER 9

According to author James J. Lachard:

- People grow bored of being children, are in a rush to grow up, and then long to be young again.
- People sacrifice their health to make money, and then spend their money to restore or save their health.
- People worry about the future, forget about the present, and live most of their lives in the past.

Try to live fully in the present today — for yourself and for your customers.

NOVEMBER 10

Great service isn't about you and what you like. It is about what your customers need and want.

NOVEMBER 11

Why are you and your organization working to improve customer experience? Is it to fix a specific problem? Is it to regain market share? Is it to increase revenue by encouraging your happy customers to buy more? Make sure you understand the "why" behind your and your organization's efforts to improve customer experience.

NOVEMBER 12

The only way to significantly improve customer experience is at the individual level. At every customer interaction, each employee must decide whether he or she will deliver genuine, compassionate care. What will you decide?

NOVEMBER 13

Don't be afraid to take a stand. Early in my career, I watched a supervisor at the hotel where I worked refuse three-quarters of a big produce delivery. Things just weren't up to her standards. The delivery driver was furious, but my supervisor stood her ground. She accepted only the items that met her quality expectations. From that day forward, that food-supply company delivered only the freshest produce to our hotel — all because one person took a stand to accept only the best!

NOVEMBER 14

Are there organizational rules or policies that stand in the way of delivering a great customer experience? What hurdles and roadblocks do you have to work around to do the right thing? Talk with your team about what's getting in the way.

NOVEMBER 15

How effective you are during a customer interaction depends heavily on the speed of your tactical and situational awareness — in other words, how quickly you can figure out what is happening. This awareness, in turn, depends heavily on listening. During each customer interaction, perform ultra-focused, unwavering, Olympic-level listening.

NOVEMBER 16

When delivering awesome customer experience, don't just learn something new; *create* something new. Sweep aside any doubts you have about your ability to innovate. Tinker. Try something different. Continuously test new approaches to see which result in the best customer experience.

NOVEMBER 17

You know all those customer measures your organization has created to quantify performance? Step back from them for a moment. Organizations sometimes overdose on data. Underlying that blizzard of information are real customers with real emotions. Don't lose the trees for the forest. In the end, just one thing matters: Was your customer's experience excellent?

NOVEMBER 18

As you interact with a customer, that person receives hundreds of instantaneous impressions from you and your organization. These form the whole of what that customer experiences. When skillfully managed, every moment is an opportunity to create and deepen experience.

NOVEMBER 19

Great-attitude guru Jeffrey Gitomer recommends that you tell yourself the following things before facing a customer:

- "I am the friendliest person in the world."
- "I am the most helpful person in the world."
- "I love to serve."
- "I don't prejudge or put anyone down."
- "I will ask before I tell."
- "I will be memorable."

A little positive self-talk won't kill you!

NOVEMBER 20

You make two statements to a customer before you even open your mouth through your appearance and how you carry yourself. Before anything else, make sure you *look* like you care.

NOVEMBER 21

Customers have three dimensions: how they feel, what they're thinking, and what they will spend. Unfortunately, many organizations seem to care only about this last one. Many customer-satisfaction issues stem from this one basic error. It's not enough to deliver what the customer wants to buy. You must also ask yourself, "How does my customer feel right now? What is he thinking?"

NOVEMBER 22

Most customer interactions are based on customer needs. Still, you might also want to think about the following:

- The customer's wants
- The customer's feelings
- The customer's level of confidence in what he or she is trying to accomplish
- The customer's history with you and your organization's products and services

NOVEMBER 23

Treat every customer equally well.
Always.

NOVEMBER 24

No surprises for your customers! Don't introduce new processes, policies, or procedures without giving your customers plenty of notice. Sometimes, even the slightest changes can leave customers upset and out of sorts. Often, what causes customer frustration is not *what* is changed, but the *way* it is changed. Give your customers time to adjust to new ways of doing things.

NOVEMBER 25

A great customer service representative always takes more than her share of the blame when something goes wrong. She also takes less than her share of the credit when things go right.

NOVEMBER 26

According to many animal trainers, rewarding desired behaviors will help to eliminate undesired ones. People are similarly programmable. That's why you should praise customers when they do the right thing. Try saying something like, "You were smart to do XYZ. I've never heard of a customer doing that before." Or, "Doing XYZ saved us a lot of time in placing this order. Thanks!"

NOVEMBER 27

Never speak ill of one customer to another. It's a no-win situation. At best, your second customer will find it off-putting. At worst, that customer will assume you talk about *every* customer that way — including her! Both outcomes are bad.

NOVEMBER 28

Use your power carefully. Yes, you may
have policies and procedures on your
side. You may even have the "right" to
take a certain action. But remember, the
best customer leaders use their
authority in a restrained manner. They
never flaunt it in front of their
customers.

NOVEMBER 29

When you give a customer your complete focus, you grant that person dignity. Today, try giving a few customers your undivided attention. If you're working with then in person, face them. Silence your phone. Don't look at your phone, tablet, or computer. Don't let anything interrupt you. Listen before you speak. And when you do speak, rephrase what you just heard. Then compare these interactions with ones during which you multi-tasked. Notice a difference?

NOVEMBER 30

It's good if customers like you…and it's great if they feel that you like them, too. But be warned: Liking your customers is something you can't fake. If you don't like working with customers, they'll know.

DECEMBER

DECEMBER 1

Do you plan to stay in your current job forever? Probably not. Still, you should strive to be the very best that you can be at your present role. There's nothing wrong with setting your sights down the road for your next position; just don't forget to do a killer job at the one you occupy today.

DECEMBER 2

Be confident during your customer interactions. After all, you've earned the right to be in your current job. Take pride in your role and in your ability to change the trajectory of a customer's experience.

DECEMBER 3

You won't win them all. The question is, can you lose graciously? Sometimes, there is absolutely nothing you can do to turn around a hopeless situation. When that happens, you must use the most powerful nine words in the English language: "I (or we) have made a mistake and I am sorry."

DECEMBER 4

Customers are protective of their privacy — and rightfully so! Make sure you do everything you can to keep their personal information safe and secure.

DECEMBER 5

Recently, my seatmate on a Southwest Airlines flight asked the flight attendant for a second packet of pretzels. She gave him some good-natured rubbing about his appetite. Then, two minutes later, she handed him a full bag of pretzel packets—about 100 servings! "Happy now?" she said with a smile. My seatmate laughed—and so did everyone else who witnessed the exchange. Can you have some fun with *your* customers today?

DECEMBER 6

Ill-chosen words can bring any conversation or customer transaction to a standstill—and it can be very difficult to get things moving again. Before you open your mouth, take a moment to remember that you're interacting with a feeling, thinking, emotional human being. Choose your words carefully. This might be the last time you see or interact with this customer.

DECEMBER 7

Nothing feels worse than someone acting indifferent toward you. But if you work in customer service, you've probably found that it's pretty easy to feel indifferent about your customers. I mean, who wants to deal with the real and raw emotions of another human being? But as the great writer Elie Wiesel noted, "Indifference reduces the other to an abstraction" — and that's *not* how you want to think about your customers. Be fully present with your customers and to recognize that each one of them is a real-live person.

DECEMBER 8

We all know what a heavy sales pitch sounds and feels like. Someone tells you how all your problems will be solved if you just buy their product or service. Not good. One key to great customer relationships is trust. One way to establish trust is to be honest about what your product or service can — and can't — do. If it's not in your customer's best interest to buy a product or service, say so. Yes, this kind of transparency might hurt you in the short term. But if you're in the customer experience business for the long haul, your customers will remember your sincerity and integrity forever.

DECEMBER 9

If you truly have your customers' best interests at heart, they will know that you're looking out for them. Don't hedge your answers. Be straight, simple, and clear.

DECEMBER 10

To deliver great customer experience, you have to take some initiative. That means doing things differently. After all, if you continue to do the same thing the same way, you're going to get the same outcome over and over again. It also means doing more than what is expected of you. Just meeting the job description is not going to get you where you need to go. You want extraordinary results, right? So be extraordinary!

DECEMBER 11

Take pride in your professional appearance. Your look will speak volumes about you before you even think of opening your mouth.

DECEMBER 12

If a customer is upset or angry with you, chances are it's not because you've caused that person physical harm. Rather, it is because you have injured him or her emotionally. You have hurt the person's feelings — his or her sensitive spirit and ego.

Customers feel more than they think. Until you're willing (and able) to interact with your customers at an emotional level, you'll never succeed in delivering truly awesome customer experience. Remember: Nothing beats simple human kindness. Nothing.

DECEMBER 13

According to psychologist Daniel Kahneman, when we are in a normal state of mind, we have intuitive feelings and opinions about almost everything that comes our way. That means we tend to like or dislike customers long before we know anything about them. And we trust or distrust their motives long before we know why. We jump to conclusions without realizing it. We give too much credence to what history we bring to the interaction than to the facts in front of us. Before you begin your next customer interaction, pause to put your history and assumptions in check.

DECEMBER 14

When working with a customer to solve a problem, always offer at least two legitimate solutions. Customers like the idea of having a choice. If you need help coming up with alternatives, ask yourself what you would do if you couldn't offer the typical solution.

DECEMBER 15

Is there someone on your team (or elsewhere) who's better at delivering some aspect of customer experience than you are? Is there some reason you haven't sat down with that person to pick his or her brain? (That's a hint.)

DECEMBER 16

Have you ever seen a small customer problem that *could* develop into something big, but you didn't do anything to stop it? Odds are, when everything was said and done, you probably wished you had nipped the problem in the bud instead of letting it get out of hand.

To quote the Department of Homeland Security, if you see something, say something. When you detect a problem at the very earliest stages of its life cycle, you have been given a gift: the opportunity to kill it before it grows bigger. Today would be an excellent day to bring some problem you've seen to someone else's attention.

DECEMBER 17

Are you hiring? Or are you looking to get hired in a customer experience role? Here are the top attributes that best-in-class customer service organizations look for in new talent:

- **Confidence:** Trusting your own judgment and resourcefulness
- **Positivity:** Having optimism and being able to see the good in any situation, no matter how bad
- **Tolerance:** Accepting differences in other people and their ideas
- **Empathy:** Being able to see the situation from the customer's point of view

DECEMBER 18

One day, a dog fell into a well. His owner couldn't figure out how to get him out. Finally, the owner decided that the dog had lived a long, good life, so he should just bury the dog in the well.

The man called his neighbors to help him bury the dog. They all grabbed shovels and began the sad task. At first, the dog barked and whimpered. Then it fell quiet.

After a while, the man peeked over the edge of the well and was amazed at what he saw. As each shovelful of dirt hit the dog, the dog shook it off and took a step up. A short while later, the man and his neighbors were astonished to see the dog jump out of the now-shallow well.

Sooner or later, customers (or just life in general) will dump all over you. To get out of the hole, shake off the stuff that's raining down on you and start climbing.

DECEMBER 19

Recently, I went to a new restaurant with my wife and our three daughters, aged eight, fourteen, and fifteen. When we arrived, the hostess took a quick look us and said, "So, three adult menus and two kid menus?"

Seems harmless enough, right? And to most of us, it was. Our eight-year-old couldn't have cared less. The fifteen-year-old, who is tall for her age, wasn't surprised to be labeled as an adult. But our fourteen-year-old, who is short for her age, was hopping mad. She sees herself as an adult, and desperately wants others to do the same.

Be cautious of careless categorizations and assumptions. Even though the food was good, we've never been back to that restaurant!

DECEMBER 20

Here is the perfect way to introduce yourself:

- Brief is best. Provide the absolute least that someone needs to know. You can reveal more later.
- Focus entirely on the customer. Smile. Make eye contact. Smile. Remember everything the customer says in the first minute. Smile. Did I mention smile?
- When you speak, use the customer's name and repeat something he or she just told you. Remember: This is all about the customer. Not you.

DECEMBER 21

Psychological research suggests that people experience thousands of interactive moments every day. The quality of your customer's day is based on whether these moments are positive, negative, or neutral. What type of moments are you delivering to your customer?

DECEMBER 22

According to famed psychologist Sidney Jourard, more than eighty-five percent of a human being's overall happiness comes from positive interactions with other people. So when you're dealing with a customer, make sure the interaction is a positive one. It could make a difference in that person's overall happiness. (No pressure!)

DECEMBER 23

Do an experiment today. Pretend you're a customer, with no knowledge of how things in your organization work. Then pretend you, the customer, have a problem. See what happens when you move through your organization's problem-recovery process. If you encounter processes that don't work or are too difficult for customers to navigate, fix them.

DECEMBER 24

The value of a sensitive, thoughtful approach in your customer relationships is immeasurable. And it works at home, too. Over the next couple of days, try some of your customer experience relationship skills on your boyfriend, girlfriend, spouse, children, parents, neighbors, and friends. I promise, it will make your holidays happier!

DECEMBER 25

Customer engagement doesn't take a holiday. Even when you're stuck working the late shift, the early shift, or a holiday shift, you still have to deliver great customer experience. Most businesses and organizations staff down for the holidays; if you're in charge of staffing, make sure you have adequate coverage to deliver the experience you intend.

DECEMBER 26

Generally speaking, your customer should never see storerooms, trash areas, work hallways, or paper-piled desks. Slower times of the year are a great time to clean up and organize workspaces that customers might potentially see.

DECEMBER 27

Does your workspace truly welcome your customer? Here are some ways to create a welcoming environment:

- Leave your door open.
- Offer comfortable seating.
- Ensure that your desk or work area does not create a physical barrier between you and your customer.
- Display tasteful decorations, photographs of people, and/or plants.

Conversely, here are some things you'll want to avoid:

- Dirty or plastic chairs
- Files or other paperwork stacked in the seating area
- Magazines that are more than a month old
- A half-eaten sandwich from last week
- A tattered Farrah Fawcett poster

Remember, both you and your work environment create an impression!

DECEMBER 28

Got a name tag? Make sure it's clean and spotless, and wear it. Always! If you have a choice, wear it on your breast, on the same side as your dominant hand. So, if you're right-handed, wear it over your right breast. That way, if you're gesturing with your right hand as you speak, customers will be drawn to look at your name. One more thing: Don't ever wear someone else's name tag. It's very bad karma!

DECEMBER 29

If you work with customers, you must know how and when to shake hands. As to the how, keep these points in mind:

- Be firm. No loose-gripped, cold fish hands.
- Make sure your hands are clean and dry.
- Don't miss! Look at the junction of the thumb and finger of the hand you're about to shake.
- Quickly release the person's hand. Two pumps and you're done.
- No crushers. Prove your strength some other way.

So when should you shake someone's hand?

- When you're introduced
- When saying goodbye
- When making a bet (but you'd better be good for it!)

Oh, and never shake hands in a restroom, when someone has his or her hands full, or while sitting.

DECEMBER 30

Forgive and forget. Customers will wrong you—sometimes repeatedly. Most of the time, their bad behavior isn't personal. Don't let anger eat you up. Be the bigger person. This doesn't mean that you should be subjected to repeated and offensive abuse. In those situations, get help—*quick*.

DECEMBER 31

As American Poet Laureate Maya Angelou wrote:

> You alone are enough.
> You have nothing to prove to anybody.
> Be yourself. Trust your gut. You're doing just great!

Have a great year!

Made in the USA
Lexington, KY
08 April 2018